Space

Exploring Space

Charlotte Guillain

H www.heinemannlibrary.co.uk
Visit our website to find out more information about Heinemann Library books.

To order:
☎ Phone 44 (0) 1865 888066
📄 Send a fax to 44 (0) 1865 314091
💻 Visit the Heinemann Bookshop at www.heinemannlibrary.co.uk to browse our catalogue and order online.

Heinemann Library is an imprint of Capstone Global Library Limited, a company incorporated in England and Wales having its registered office at 7 Pilgrim Street, London, EC4V 6LB – Registered company number: 6695582

Heinemann is a registered trademark of Pearson Education Limited, under licence to Capstone Global Library Limited

Edited by Sian Smith, Rebecca Rissman, and Charlotte Guillain
Designed by Joanna Hinton-Malivoire
Picture research by Tracy Cummins and Heather Mauldin
Production by Duncan Gilbert
Originated by Heinemann Library
Printed and bound in China by Leo Paper Group

ISBN 978 0 431 19391 5
13 12 11 10 09
10 9 8 7 6 5 4 3 2 1

British Library Cataloguing in Publication Data
Guillain, Charlotte
   Exploring space. - (Acorn plus)
   1. Astronautics - Juvenile literature 2. Outer space - Exploration - Juvenile literature
   I. Title
   629.4

Acknowledgements
We would like to thank the following for permission to reproduce photographs: Getty Images pp.**5, 9, 10** (©Stocktrek), **22** (©William Radcliffe); NASA pp.**14, 16** (©GRIN), **18** (©Edwin E. Buzz Aldrin), **7** (©SOHO); Photo Researchers Inc pp. **15, 19** (©Science Source/NASA), **4** (©Chris Butler), **21** (©David A. Hardy), **8** (©Detlev van Ravenswaay), **20** (©John Sanford), **13** (©Mark Garlick); Photolibrary pp.**6, 11** (©Albert Klein), **12** (©The Stocktrek Corp); ©UPI p.**17** (©NASA)

Front cover and back cover photographs reproduced with permission of NASA (©GRIN).

Every effort has been made to contact copyright holders of material reproduced in this book. Any omissions will be rectified in subsequent printings if notice is given to the publishers.

Contents

Some words are shown in bold, **like this**. They are explained in "Words to know" on page 23.

Space

Up above the sky is space. In space there are **stars**, **moons**, and **planets**.

We live on Earth. Earth is a planet in space.

What are planets?

Planets are very large, round objects that are in space. Some planets are made of rock. Some planets are made of **gas**.

the Sun

Planets move around, or **orbit**, a **star**. Earth orbits a star called the Sun.

The Solar System

Earth

Earth is not the only **planet** that **orbits** the Sun. There are seven other planets that orbit the Sun, too.

The Sun and the eight planets that orbit the Sun are called the **Solar System**.

Pluto

People used to count nine **planets**. People called Pluto the ninth planet, but it was very small.

Pluto

People found more small objects like Pluto in space.
These are called **dwarf planets**. Pluto is one of many
dwarf planets.

Moons

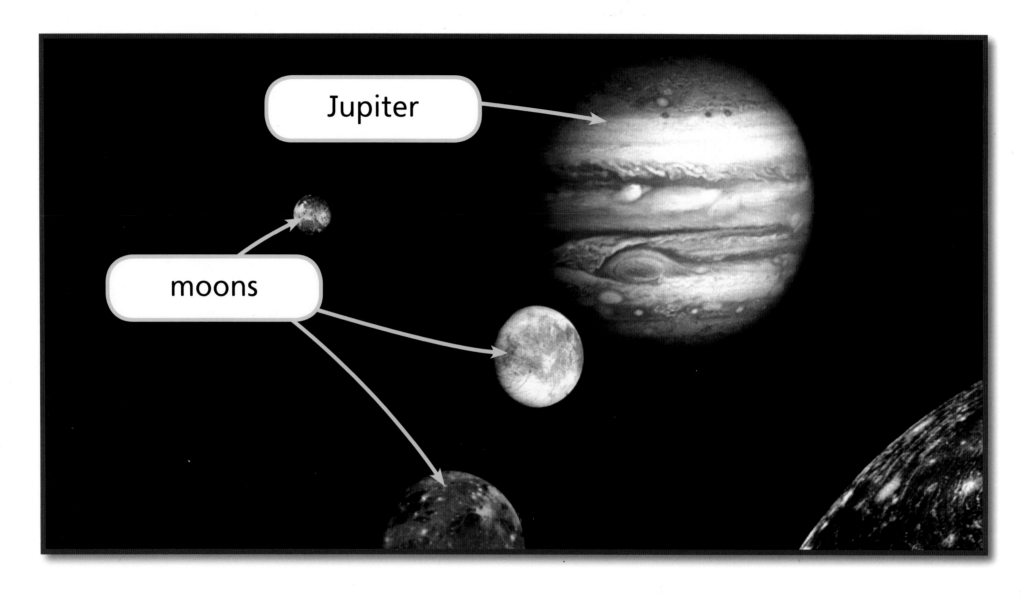

Jupiter

moons

Some **planets** have **moons**. Moons **orbit** planets.

the Moon

the Sun

Earth has one moon. The Moon is dark. You can see the Moon at night because light from the Sun shines on it.

Space travel

People have travelled into space. First people travelled into space in **rockets**. Now people travel in smaller **space shuttles** that look like aeroplanes.

People who travel into space are called **astronauts**.
Astronauts are scientists who study things in space.
Astronauts spend a lot of time on Earth studying
and training.

Astronauts have to wear special suits in space when they are not inside the **space shuttle**. The suits keep them cool when they are in the Sun's heat and warm when they are in darkness. The suit also gives them air to breathe.

Astronauts float when they are in space. This is called being **weightless**. Even food and drink can float away!

Where have we travelled to?

Astronauts have been to the Moon. They studied the rocks and dust on the surface of the Moon.

People have not travelled to other **planets** yet. But people have sent **robots** and machines to take pictures of other planets. People are studying Mars with machines.

Other stars, other galaxies

The Sun is just one **star** in space. We can see many stars in the night sky and many more when we look through **telescopes**. Most stars in the sky have their own **planets** orbiting round them.

the Milky Way

Stars make up a **galaxy**. Our galaxy is called the Milky Way. There are many other galaxies in space. Where will people go to next?

How to remember the planets

Here is a way to help you remember the order of the **planets** from the Sun.

My Very Energetic Monkey Just Stepped Upon Noodles.

My   **M** = Mercury

Very   **V** = Venus

Energetic   **E** = Earth

Monkey   **M** = Mars

Just   **J** = Jupiter

Stepped   **S** = Saturn

Upon   **U** = Uranus

Noodles   **N** = Neptune

Words to know

astronaut   scientist who studies things in space

dwarf planet   object in space smaller than a planet. Pluto is a dwarf planet.

galaxy   group of stars. The galaxy we live in is called the Milky Way.

gas   substance that is not solid or liquid and moves around like air

moon   object in space that orbits a planet

orbit   move around

planet   large object in space that orbits a star

robot   machine that can do things like a person

rocket   vehicle used to travel into space

space shuttle   vehicle used to travel into space that looks similar to an aeroplane

Solar System   the Sun and the eight planets that orbit it

star   huge ball of gas that gives out heat and light

telescope   tool that makes far away things look bigger so that we can see them more easily

weightless   floating

Index

Notes for parents and teachers

Before reading

Talk to the children about the Solar System. Look at picture on page 9. Ask the children which planets they think will be hotter than Earth and which cooler. Why?

After reading

- Use three children to demonstrate the movement of the Moon round Earth and Earth round the Sun. One child will be the Sun and will stand in the middle of the room. The second child will be the planet Earth. That child will need to spin slowly and, at the same time, move in a wide circle (orbit) around the Sun. The third child will be the Moon. The Moon needs to move in a circle around Earth but always stay facing Earth. Talk to the children about a day (one turn of Earth); a month (the time it takes for the Moon to move around Earth); a year (the time it takes Earth to move around the Sun).

- Make a space rocket. You will need: 1 paper towel tube; foil; thin card; tissue paper in red, orange, and yellow; tape; scissors. Wrap the tube in foil, leaving about 8cm loose at the top. Use sticky tape to fix the foil. Shape the top of the foil into a point. Cut out a circle from the card about 15cm in diameter. Cut the circle in half, and then half again. Fold over one of the straight edges on each quarter to create tabs that will be used to attach the fins to the rocket. Use sticky tape to fix the fins around the bottom of the rocket. Cut streamers of tissue paper about 2cm wide by 25cm long and fix these inside the bottom of the rocket.